The IMPORTANT Story EVER TOLD

WorldServe
MINISTRIES

Creation – Adam and Eve

Bible Reference: Genesis 1, 2

God said, "Let us make people in our image, to be like ourselves." And the LORD God formed a man's body from the dust of the ground and breathed into it the breath of life. And the man became a living person.

"Dust?"

"Right, Tony. God can do anything!"

Then God said, "It is not good for the man to be alone. I will make a partner who will help him." So the LORD God caused Adam to fall into a deep sleep. He took one of Adam's ribs and made a woman from the rib.

God brought the woman, Eve, to Adam as his wife.

At the center of the garden God placed the tree of life and the tree of the knowledge of good and evil. But the LORD God gave the man this warning: "You may freely eat any fruit in the garden except fruit from the tree of the knowledge of good and evil. If you eat of its fruit, you will surely die."

Adam and Eve lived in the garden and they were very happy. They were close to God and enjoyed being with him. But one day...

Adam and Eve Sin

Bible Reference: Genesis 3

Satan, God's enemy, disguised himself as a serpent. He didn't want Adam and Eve to be with God and obey him.

He asked Eve, "Did God really say you must not eat any of the fruit in the garden?"

She told him, "It's only the fruit from the tree at the center of the garden that we are not allowed to eat. God says we must not eat it or even touch it, or we will die."

"You won't die!" the serpent hissed. "You will become just like God."

The woman was convinced. The fruit looked so fresh and delicious, and it would make her so wise! So she...

"NO! Don't eat it, Eve!"

"Good advice, Tony. But she did, and so did Adam."

Suddenly, they were afraid. They hid from God when he came to walk in the garden. They had sinned by choosing to disobey God. So he sent them away – out of the Garden of Eden.

God loved Adam and Eve. He wanted them to have a choice, to choose for themselves to love and obey him. But they chose to disobey God. They didn't know how awful separation from God would be.

And, because they chose to sin, everyone who came after them was born sinful and separated from God, too.

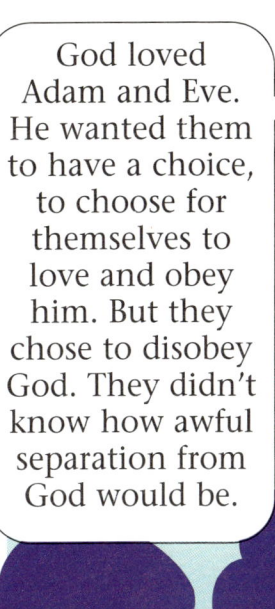

You mean we can't be with God because of them? That's not fair!

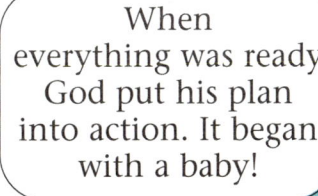

Not only because of them, Tony. We all sin when we do wrong things. But don't worry. God had a wonderful plan to bring us back to him. He just needed one perfect person.

When everything was ready God put his plan into action. It began with a baby!

Jesus is Born

Bible Reference: Matthew 1, Luke 2

God gave Mary his own Son as a baby. He chose Joseph to help Mary look after him. Because the baby was God's Son, he was born without sin.

An angel of the Lord appeared to Joseph in a dream. The angel said, "Mary will have a son, and you are to name him Jesus, for he will save his people from their sins." ("Jesus" means the Lord saves.)

Just before the baby was born, Joseph and Mary had

to go to Bethlehem.

While they were there, Mary gave birth to her first child, a son.

God sent angels to tell people about his Son's birth. They came to see this amazing event: God's Son born as a baby!

"Jesus grew up like you kids."

"Did he go to school, Dad? And play?"

"Yes, Tony. He also obeyed his parents, and was obedient to his real Father, God. And he never sinned!"

Jesus the Teacher

Bible Reference: Luke 2, Matthew 22, John 3

When he was 12 years old, Jesus was in Jerusalem with the teachers.

He was in the temple discussing deep questions with them. And all who heard him were amazed at his understanding and his answers.

Jesus grew both in height and in wisdom, and he was loved by God and by all who knew him.

When he was 30, Jesus started to teach and preach. He taught that God cares how people think and act. And he said,"**You must love the Lord your God with all your heart, all your soul, and all your mind.' This is the first and greatest commandment. A second is equally important: 'Love your neighbor as yourself.'"**

Jesus told about God's wonderful plan to bring us back to him.

He said, **"God so loved the world that he gave his only Son, so that everyone who believes in him will not perish but have eternal life."**

"I believe in Jesus, Dad!"

"That's great, Deanna!"

Jesus the Healer

Bible Reference: Matthew 4, 9

Jesus also helped people see what God is like. He showed them God loves them. One way he did this was by healing every kind of sickness and disease.

The sick were soon coming to be healed. And whatever their illness and pain, or if they were possessed by demons, or were epileptics, or were paralyzed – Jesus healed them all.

One time, a ruler got down on his knees in front of Jesus.

"My daughter has just died," he said, "but you can bring her back to life again if you just come and lay your hand upon her."

Jesus went and took the girl by the hand, and she stood up!

"Wow! Jesus really healed people, Dad?"

"Yes, Tony. Nothing is too hard for him!"

Jesus the Miracle Worker

Bible Reference: Matthew 14, John 6

"Jesus did other wonderful and amazing things. He calmed storms and walked on water!"

"That must have been exciting!"

"It was, Tony. Another time, a crowd of more than 5000 followed Jesus to a distant place. His friends and followers, the disciples, wanted to send the crowd away because it was past supper time."

Jesus replied, "That isn't necessary — you feed them."

Andrew spoke up. "There's a youngster here with five barley loaves and two fish! But what good is that with this huge crowd?"

Jesus took the loaves, gave thanks to God, and passed them out to the people. Afterward he did the same with the fish. And they all ate until they were full!

"Now gather the leftovers," Jesus told his disciples, "so that nothing is wasted."

There were only five barley loaves to start with, but twelve baskets were filled with the pieces of bread the people did not eat!

"There were more leftovers than the food they started with?"

"Right, Deanna. Jesus was teaching them God can meet all their needs. He'll do the same for us when we ask him."

Jesus and the Children

Bible Reference: Matthew 19, Mark 10

"Jesus showed people that God loves children. He healed them, let them help him (like the boy with the food), and even raised them from the dead!"

Some children were brought to Jesus so he could lay his hands on them and pray for them. The disciples told them not to bother him.

When Jesus saw what was happening, he said, "Let the children come to me. Don't stop them! Anyone who

doesn't have their kind of faith will never get into the Kingdom of God." Then he took the children into his arms and placed his hands on their heads and blessed them.

"I want to be blessed by Jesus, too!"

"You can be, Tony. Jesus is the same today and he loves children just as much.

"Not everyone liked him, 'though. What he did and taught made the religious leaders angry. They were jealous that the people liked him so much. So they planned to get rid of him."

Jesus' Arrest and Trial

Bible Reference: Luke 22, John 19

"One night, when Jesus was talking to his friends, the religious leaders sent a crowd with clubs and swords."

The disciples exclaimed, "Lord, should we fight? We brought the swords!" And one of them slashed at a servant and cut off his right ear.

But Jesus said, "Don't resist any more." And he touched the place where the man's ear had been and healed him.

"Jesus healed one of his enemies?"

"Yes, Deanna. He loves everyone."

They grabbed Jesus and arrested him. They took him to the ruler of the area, Pilate, and put him on trial. The soldiers beat Jesus, put thorns on his head, and made fun of him. Then Pilate spoke to the people.

"I am going to bring him out to you now, but understand clearly that I find him not guilty."

"Away with him," they yelled. "Crucify him!"

Then Pilate gave Jesus to them to be crucified.

"But he didn't do anything wrong! That's not fair!"

"Right, Tony. But remember, God had a plan."

Jesus Dies on the Cross

Bible Reference: Luke 23

"They nailed Jesus to the cross."

Jesus said, "Father, forgive these people, because they don't know what they are doing."

Two others, both criminals, were executed with him. One of the criminals hanging beside him scoffed, "So you're the Messiah, are you?" (Messiah is another name for the Son of God.) **"Prove it by saving yourself – and us, too, while you're at it!"**

But the other criminal protested, "Don't you fear God even when you are dying? We deserve to die for our evil deeds, but this man hasn't done anything wrong." Then he said, "Jesus, remember me when you come into your Kingdom."

Jesus replied, "I assure you, today you will be with me in paradise."

"He got to be with Jesus after he died?"

"Right, Deanna!"

"Later, Jesus cried out to his Father, God, and died."

"Hey, is Jesus the person in God's plan?"

"Right, Tony. God sent his own perfect Son, Jesus. And he died to take the punishment for our sins."

Jesus is Alive

Bible Reference: Matthew 28, Luke 24

Jesus' body was put in a tomb by his friends.
Early on the first day of the week two women went to the tomb.

Suddenly there was a great earthquake, because an angel of the Lord came down from heaven and rolled aside the stone from the tomb.

"Don't be afraid." he said. "I know you are looking for Jesus, who was crucified. He isn't here! He has been raised from the dead, just as he said would happen.

Now go quickly and tell his disciples."

"That's the best part!"

"Right, Tony! After he'd paid for our sins God raised him from the dead. That was God's plan all along.

Later, as the disciples were talking about it, **Jesus himself was suddenly standing there among them. He said, "Peace be with you." But the whole group was terribly frightened, thinking they were seeing a ghost!**

"Why are you frightened?" he asked. "Look at my hands. Look at my feet. You can see that it's really me. Touch me and make sure that I am not a ghost!"

Where is Jesus Today?

Bible Reference: John 16, Acts 1

"Jesus was with his disciples for many weeks."

"They must have been happy!"

"Yes, but where's Jesus now?"

"Good question, Deanna."

Jesus said, **"It is actually best for you that I go away, because if I don't, the Holy Spirit won't come. If I do go away, he will come, because I will send him to you."**

If you prayed with Tony, you've made the most important decision and started the greatest adventure of all. Write your name and the date here so you'll always remember:

"I, _____, became God's

child today." Date: _____

To continue on in your greatest adventure:

- Pray. Talk to God from your heart about anything, anytime, anywhere.
- Get a Bible and begin reading it. Try starting with the book of Mark, then Acts and James. Then just keep reading.
- Tell your friends what has happened to you. They can become God's children too.
- Find a local church where they love Jesus and where the Bible is taught. You'll meet more of God's children and learn about God.

When Jesus had finished speaking with the disciples, they watched him rise into the sky and disappear into a cloud. Two angels told them, **"Jesus has been taken away from you into heaven. And someday, just as you saw him go, he will return!"**

One day Jesus will come back for all God's children. That's everyone who believes Jesus died for them, and has been forgiven. We will be with him forever. Nothing will ever separate us from God's love again!

I want to be God's child, so I can be with him.

That's great, Tony! This is the most important decision you'll ever make! The Bible tells us our sin separates us from God. And it says, "If you confess with your mouth that Jesus is Lord and believe in your heart that God raised him from the dead, you will be saved. For it is by believing in your heart that you are made right with God, and it is by confessing with your mouth that you are saved." *Romans 10:9-10*

I can say that! I really do believe in Jesus!

Then let's tell God. He's always listening, Tony. He hears our prayers and answers us. Say this prayer with me.

Dear God, I know I'm a sinner. I made wrong choices and did bad things. I'm sorry. Please forgive me. I know your Son, Jesus, died for my sins and I believe you raised him from the dead. I want Jesus to be my Lord. Thank you for loving me and making me your child. Now, please fill me with your Holy Spirit, so I'll have all the strength I need to obey you. Amen.

Wow! I'm God's child now, aren't I?

Absolutely!

Now, to get to know God better, be sure to talk to him in prayer and read about him in his book, the Bible. God speaks to you through the Bible and tells you about the important things he has for you to do.

What are they, Dad?

To love God, tell people about Jesus, and show them God's love and power.

Jesus told his followers, "Go and make disciples... Teach them to obey all the commands I have given you. And be sure of this: I am with you always." *Matthew 28:19-20*